*Life is Learning,
Learning is Life.*

UN SCHOOLING
journal

Jennifer Althaus

© Jennifer Althaus 2021

Jennifer Althaus asserts the moral right to be identified as the author of 'UnSchooling Journal'

Cover design and typeset by Green Avenue Design

ISBN: 978-0-6450004-1-2

All rights reserved. No part of this publication may be reproduced, stored in a retrieval system, or transmitted, in any form or by any means, electronic, mechanical, photocopying, recording or otherwise, without the prior permission of the publishers.

Cilento Publishing, Sydney, Australia
www.cilentopublishing.com

This journal is also available as a printable PDF so you can make your own working folder.
You can find it at jenniferalthaus.com.au

About this journal

Learning does not start at the age for compulsory school enrolment and end when the formal schooling years are over. We are learning from the day we are born until the day we die. The traditional mainstream schooling system leads us to believe that learning starts when the bell rings, involves listening to the instructions of an adult and answering questions in the correct manner. Letters, numbers and gold stars become our reward. Way too many times it fails our children as they struggle to understand, fall behind and feel discouraged when they cannot achieve what is expected of them. There are no allowances for individual strengths and weaknesses.

Unschooling, a term coined by educator John Holt in the 1970's to mean learning and teaching that does not resemble school learning, is the recognition that as humans we are natural learners. It is not about doing nothing; it is about doing lots. Unschooled children learn through natural life experiences. Learning is driven by their passions and environment. By providing a learning enriched environment that is child led and focused learning is achieved. It is not a chore or something we 'must' do but part of our life. It is fun, adventurous and inviting. When we offer a child the opportunity to be in control of their learning they are empowered.

In countries where home educating is legal there is a level of reporting that must be done to meet legal requirements. This journal has been designed to be used as a record of unschooling activities that can be presented to the relevant authority. It is designed as a quick recording method filled in with one or two chosen activities each week. It can be filled in by an adult or given to the child as an activity of self-reflection. It complements the legal documents required by the overseeing government department in your area. It is not designed to stand alone.

This journal is available as a downloadable and printable PDF from
www.jenniferalthaus.com.au

How to use this journal

Yearly overview: Learning philosophy, visions and goals.

The first few pages are where you write your learning philosophy and your visions and goals. These show the necessary authorities that even though you choose not to offer any formal structured learning you are aware of why you unschool and what it means to your family. Your learning philosophy may not differ much year to year, but your goals and visions definitely will.

Your philosophy is your reason: the why behind your unschooling. What is the guiding principle? What are your beliefs? For me John Holt is my influence and the philosopher I follow, although over the 22 years of unschooling I have developed my own philosophy that fits my findings and lifestyle. The philosophical quote I have developed is that of the name of this book. When writing your learning philosophy be creative. Dig deep into the core values of your family. Ask the family to help you write a philosophy that represents all of you.

Your visions and goals are a little trickier, especially if you have more than one child and the ages vary greatly. In this situation you may wish to write one or two different goals for each child, listing them under their names. Visions and goals only need to be short and in point form.

Your vision is general. A vision is a statement; one or two sentences describing what you see your family achieving. Your goals are your vision in more detail. How is your vision going to be achieved?

Your vision may be for days filled with adventure, personal growth and developmental achievement. An example of a goal based on this vision may be for your child to use his or her surrounding environment to expand their understanding of the written word and numbers whilst developing life skills. The activities you record in this journal will complement your goals, showing that you have provided a rich environment integral to your plan.

Notes of Interest

This is a place to list anything you like. If your child/ren have any special needs list them here. Note any outcomes from the previous year that your child/ren struggled with or achieved that may influence their learning for this year. List any therapies they are undergoing, sports or community groups they attend.

List anything you feel is important to your child's learning outcomes or anything you would like to share with the registration department.

Observations throughout the year

Two pages have been left blank for you to write down anything you observe as the year progresses.

Achievements

We should always focus on the positive and not dwell on the negative. List your child's achievements and be proud of them. Have your child write their achievements on the page, owning their success. Achievements do not have to be large or academically based. Maybe they got ready for the day unaided, folded the washing or made their lunch each day for the week. Maybe they did a beautiful drawing or said thank you to the lady who served them at the shop.

Excursions

List places you visit and events you attend. This need only be in point form. You may like to include a brief line or two about what you did. Expand on these by filling out an activity page, including photos and a more in-depth presentation.

Recording activities

The top of each page has been left blank for you to add a visual record of your activity. You might choose a photo, a drawing, a sample of paperwork, a piece of nature...

Activity: Get creative and give your activity a title.

Learning areas: This sits outside of the understanding of learning in regard to unschooling but living in today's society means we must accept legislation and report in accordance with a designed curriculum. What areas of learning were undertaken when you were engaged in your activity? Areas of learning interrelate so don't just focus on one. Look at the greater picture. We cannot learn in one area without learning in others. List all areas covered.

Overview: This area is for writing what you did. This is a place to reflect on the event, process and outcome. Did you learn anything new? Did it not go as expected? Did it lead to exploring other areas? Your child may wish to fill this part out by either writing it themselves or discussing what to write with you.

I suggest keeping this book as a record of your year, sending copies of the originals for registration. It is important that we keep original copies of records of unschooling in case they are needed at a later date. It is also a record of growth over the years and a part of our children's lives.

At the back of this book there are blank pages. These have been left blank intentionally as a place for you to attach samples of work or make extra notes.

I have allowed recording space for two activities a week. As unschoolers we should not be bogged down with record keeping but instead be enjoying the wonders life offers us. If you need more record keeping space you are welcome to copy pages and attach it to the back of the book.

'Living is learning and when kids are living fully and energetically and happily they are learning a lot, even if we don't always know what it is.'

– John Holt

Yearly Overview

Learning Philosophy

UNSCHOOLING JOURNAL

Vision and goals

Notes of Interest

Notes of Interest: (contd.)

Observations throughout the year

Observations throughout the year (contd.)

Achievements

Achievements (contd.)

Excursions

Excursions (contd.)

Record of Activities

Date:

Activity:

Areas of learning:

Overview:

Date:

Activity:

Areas of learning:

Overview:

Date:

Activity:

Areas of learning:

Overview:

Date:

Activity:

Areas of learning:

Overview:

Date:

Activity:

Areas of learning:

Overview:

Date:

Activity:

Areas of learning:

Overview:

Date:

Activity:

Areas of learning:

Overview:

Date:

Activity:

Areas of learning:

Overview:

Date:

Activity:

Areas of learning:

Overview:

Date:

Activity:

Areas of learning:

Overview:

UnSchooling Journal

Date:

Activity:

Areas of learning:

Overview:

Date:

Activity:

Areas of learning:

Overview:

Date:

Activity:

Areas of learning:

Overview:

Date:

Activity:

Areas of learning:

Overview:

UNSCHOOLING JOURNAL

Date:

Activity:

Areas of learning:

Overview:

Date:

Activity:

Areas of learning:

Overview:

Date:

Activity:

Areas of learning:

Overview:

Date:

Activity:

Areas of learning:

Overview:

Date:

Activity:

Areas of learning:

Overview:

Date:

Activity:

Areas of learning:

Overview:

Date:

Activity:

Areas of learning:

Overview:

Date:

Activity:

Areas of learning:

Overview:

Date:

Activity:

Areas of learning:

Overview:

UNSCHOOLING JOURNAL

Date:

Activity:

Areas of learning:

Overview:

Date:

Activity:

Areas of learning:

Overview:

Date:

Activity:

Areas of learning:

Overview:

Date:

Activity:

Areas of learning:

Overview:

UNSCHOOLING JOURNAL

Date:

Activity:

Areas of learning:

Overview:

Date:

Activity:

Areas of learning:

Overview:

Date:

Activity:

Areas of learning:

Overview:

Date:

Activity:

Areas of learning:

Overview:

Date:

Activity:

Areas of learning:

Overview:

Date:

Activity:

Areas of learning:

Overview:

Date:

Activity:

Areas of learning:

Overview:

Date:

Activity:

Areas of learning:

Overview:

Date:

Activity:

Areas of learning:

Overview:

Date:

Activity:

Areas of learning:

Overview:

Date:

Activity:

Areas of learning:

Overview:

Date:

Activity:

Areas of learning:

Overview:

Date:

Activity:

Areas of learning:

Overview:

Date:

Activity:

Areas of learning:

Overview:

UNSCHOOLING JOURNAL

Date:

Activity:

Areas of learning:

Overview:

Date:

Activity:

Areas of learning:

Overview:

Date:

Activity:

Areas of learning:

Overview:

Date:

Activity:

Areas of learning:

Overview:

Date:

Activity:

Areas of learning:

Overview:

Date:

Activity:

Areas of learning:

Overview:

Date:

Activity:

Areas of learning:

Overview:

Date:

Activity:

Areas of learning:

Overview:

Date:

Activity:

Areas of learning:

Overview:

Date:

Activity:

Areas of learning:

Overview:

Date:

Activity:

Areas of learning:

Overview:

Date:

Activity:

Areas of learning:

Overview:

Date:

Activity:

Areas of learning:

Overview:

Date:

Activity:

Areas of learning:

Overview:

UNSCHOOLING JOURNAL

Date:

Activity:

Areas of learning:

Overview:

Date:

Activity:

Areas of learning:

Overview:

Date:

Activity:

Areas of learning:

Overview:

Date:

Activity:

Areas of learning:

Overview:

Date:

Activity:

Areas of learning:

Overview:

Date:

Activity:

Areas of learning:

Overview:

Date:

Activity:

Areas of learning:

Overview:

Date:

Activity:

Areas of learning:

Overview:

Date:

Activity:

Areas of learning:

Overview:

UNSCHOOLING JOURNAL

Date:

Activity:

Areas of learning:

Overview:

UNSCHOOLING JOURNAL

Date:

Activity:

Areas of learning:

Overview:

Date:

Activity:

Areas of learning:

Overview:

Date:

Activity:

Areas of learning:

Overview:

UNSCHOOLING JOURNAL

Date:

Activity:

Areas of learning:

Overview:

UNSCHOOLING JOURNAL

Date:

Activity:

Areas of learning:

Overview:

UNSCHOOLING JOURNAL

Date:

Activity:

Areas of learning:

Overview:

Date:

Activity:

Areas of learning:

Overview:

UNSCHOOLING JOURNAL

Date:

Activity:

Areas of learning:

Overview:

Date:

Activity:

Areas of learning:

Overview:

UNSCHOOLING JOURNAL

Date:

Activity:

Areas of learning:

Overview:

Date:

Activity:

Areas of learning:

Overview:

UNSCHOOLING JOURNAL

Date:

Activity:

Areas of learning:

Overview:

Date:

Activity:

Areas of learning:

Overview:

UnSchooling Journal

Date:

Activity:

Areas of learning:

Overview:

Date:

Activity:

Areas of learning:

Overview:

Date:

Activity:

Areas of learning:

Overview:

Date:

Activity:

Areas of learning:

Overview:

UNSCHOOLING JOURNAL

Date:

Activity:

Areas of learning:

Overview:

Date:

Activity:

Areas of learning:

Overview:

Date:

Activity:

Areas of learning:

Overview:

Date:

Activity:

Areas of learning:

Overview:

UNSCHOOLING JOURNAL

Date:

Activity:

Areas of learning:

Overview:

Date:

Activity:

Areas of learning:

Overview:

Date:

Activity:

Areas of learning:

Overview:

UNSCHOOLING JOURNAL

Date:

Activity:

Areas of learning:

Overview:

Date:

Activity:

Areas of learning:

Overview:

Date:

Activity:

Areas of learning:

Overview:

Date:

Activity:

Areas of learning:

Overview:

Date:

Activity:

Areas of learning:

Overview:

Date:

Activity:

Areas of learning:

Overview:

Date:

Activity:

Areas of learning:

Overview:

Date:

Activity:

Areas of learning:

Overview:

Date:

Activity:

Areas of learning:

Overview:

Date:

Activity:

Areas of learning:

Overview:

Date:

Activity:

Areas of learning:

Overview:

UNSCHOOLING JOURNAL

Date:

Activity:

Areas of learning:

Overview:

Date:

Activity:

Areas of learning:

Overview:

Date:

Activity:

Areas of learning:

Overview:

UNSCHOOLING JOURNAL

Date:

Activity:

Areas of learning:

Overview:

About the author

Jennifer Althaus has been part of the unschooling community for 25 years. She has three children. Two are now adults but she continues to unschool her youngest who is 13. Two of her children have autism.

Unschooling ran through Jennifer's blood way before she had children. As an early childhood educator who owned her own childcare centre, which included before and after school care, Jennifer thrived on providing a learning enriched environment for children that was as natural as possible. It was during these years she knew she would unschool her own children.

After the birth of her last child Jennifer set out with only what they could fit into a 12-foot caravan and traveled Australia with her children. It is during this time that she truly saw the strength of unschooling. As the children explored the vastness Australia has to offer they flourished both academically and personally. Memories were created that instilled a life of learning into their blood.

Jennifer currently runs her own writing and publishing consultancy business, combining business life with unschooling. She is the author of A Journey of Love, A Mother's Memoir and children's picture books. She is available to speak on all thing's unschooling, autism, assistance dogs and living a life filled with positive moments.

Contact Jennifer:

Email: oecreativeminds@gmail.com

Facebook: www.facebook.com/jenniferalthausauthor

Instagram: www.instagram.com/oecreativeminds

www.ingramcontent.com/pod-product-compliance
Lightning Source LLC
Chambersburg PA
CBHW081418300426
44109CB00019BA/2342